Solid Ground

A Devotional Journey

*21 topics designed to make you
stronger in your faith and take you
deeper in your relationship with God.*

Esther R. Milne

ISBN 978-1-954693-07-4

First edition FV-9

Cover Design by Stephen Johnson

Photos by Jonathan Milne

Author web page: **www.adevotionaljourney.com**

Published by

www.IntellectPublishing.com

"As a marriage and family counselor for over 35 years I am familiar with much when it comes to healing and restoration. How refreshing it was when I read Esther Milne's, Solid Ground. Each section of this devotional will touch your heart and challenge you as you say to yourself, "That's me!" Esther's goal is to encourage you to restore your foundation of faith and love, to stand on solid ground, which she has successfully accomplished. This book is well written, poignant, and very effective. I will use this devotional in my ministry."

Charles F. Finck M.S. Counselor, Author
Liberty Cross Ministries
As We Forgive Those-How to Forgive Others, Ourselves and God

"Esther Milne's Solid Ground comes across clearly with biblical truth, action steps, and her own personal stories. I highly recommend this short thought provoking read for anyone looking for a spot-on devotional."

Author, Linda Ray Center

"Esther answers relevant and difficult questions with simplicity and by using her own life experiences. It is an enjoyable read that will encourage a deeper walk with God . You will want to read this one over and over again!"

Tondi Curtis, Connect Church, Gulf Shores

"Reading Esther Milne's 'Solid Ground' has helped me to search many areas of my own heart. It has also opened my eyes to see things that I hadn't understood before. I highly recommend this book and am sure that it will help many people."

Eglaide Seiber Barroso, Executive Editor
The Lighthouse News

"*In Solid Ground, Esther highlights key biblical principles to effectively bring them into practical application for our daily lives using her own easily relatable experiences as a model. Those who take each lesson to heart will find a positive, encouraging journey to strengthen their spirit and help keep their feet from sliding on the shifting sands of popular cultural views or the slippery slope of ungodly thoughts and negative self-talk. A challenging yet sweet exercise to engage in!*

Peg Snyder, Passion for Life Ministries

Dedication

This book is dedicated to Dr. Alicia Barton and to many unnamed family members, friends, teachers, mentors and just those folks I've met along the way, who have sowed into my life and have helped me to become who I am today.

I am so very thankful to you all!

Preface

I'm writing this devotional from Foley, Alabama just a few miles from the beautiful beaches of the Gulf Coast. I moved here with my husband, Jonathan at the end of 2016, believing that this was where the Lord was leading us for our next season of life.

Almost immediately upon arriving here, I was introduced to Dr. Alicia Barton by our Realtor, Romney, to whom I will always be grateful, and I began working with the team at the Full Armor Center not long afterwards. What a fun, vibrant and healthy place to work and the best introduction to life on the Gulf Coast!

As soon as you walk into the Full Armor Center you see Dr. Alicia's mission written in large lettering on the wall; "To save as many lives as possible, especially children". I was fresh from the mission field having spent two months ministering in South America before moving here, and this was definitely a vision I could get behind.

As part of the team, we started a weekly discipleship Bible study group open to any of the patients and community who wanted to attend, and we called it 'Solid Ground'. The center was named prophetically from Ephesians 6:13 which says:

"Therefore, put on the full armor of God, so that when the day of evil comes, you may be able to stand your ground, and after you have done everything, to stand." NIV

The armor is important. We have a responsibility to protect ourselves with the tools that God has given us but then it's equally important to make sure that we're standing on solid ground, so that we can stand and not give in to the pressures of life. That's how we came up with the name Solid Ground.

In this devotional I've put together a short collection of studies on topics that may be relevant to your life and may answer some of the questions that have been keeping you up at night. There are 21 in fact, because Alicia and other experts will tell you that it takes 21 days to form a new habit, but if it takes you 21 weeks, that's fine by me. The habit that I hope you form is to spend more time experiencing the presence of God.

I grew up in a Christian home but as a teenager I found it difficult to be in church and didn't know how to have a relationship with God. This is the reason why I have a heart to help those who are younger than me, either in the faith or in age, to navigate their relationship with God. I don't have all the answers, but I certainly know someone who does!

I dedicate this book to the memory of Dr. Alicia, who touched many lives in this Gulf Coast community. My hope is that you'll catch a glimpse of the faith that she had and as I share some of my thoughts and experiences, it will encourage you to move forward in your faith.

Solid Ground – A Devotional Journey

CONTENTS

Solid Ground

A Devotional Journey

21 topics designed to make you stronger in your faith and take you deeper in your relationship with God.

Chapter 1

Solid Ground

L et's start at the beginning with the title of this devotional and look at our foundation and why it's always important to consider the ground we are standing on. I'm going to do that by telling you a story from my life.

It took place in 2010 when Jonathan and I were in Santiago, Chile, for a couple of months looking after a church that had been planted by our church in the US. Very early one morning we experienced one of the strongest earthquakes that has ever been recorded on the Richter scale. In pitch darkness we heard the sounds of things falling around us with no idea what the damage would be or if we would even survive. You see, I grew up in England where we experience wind and rain but not a lot of extreme weather or natural disasters. My experience of earthquakes had been limited to seeing TV reports with images of buildings reduced to piles of rubble, in faraway countries.

We had left the building and sought shelter with some friends after the earthquake happened and we returned the next day to survey the scene. I was amazed that such a violent event had caused little to no structural damage to the building. I learned that in a city such as this, buildings are designed and constructed to withstand earthquakes. It's not a question of if they happen, but when they will happen.

In the Gospel of Matthew, Jesus told a story where He compared a wise man, who built his house on the rock with a foolish man who built his house on the sand. In today's world with all our advanced learning and technology, you may wonder why anyone would be so stupid as to try building a house directly on the sand and that's why we need to go back to the context of the story in Jesus' day.

Jesus was teaching in the hilly region of Galilee, where streams would flow from the hilltops in the winter and early spring. Oftentimes the streams would overflow and flood their banks and leave beds of alluvial deposit on either side. I know very little about construction but I read that if a stranger had come to the area in the summer time, they might have been attracted by this surface that was already prepared, instead of having to build on the hard and rugged rock. It may be advantageous at first to build on the sand. You'd get ahead so much quicker … but only until those winter rains come around again with all the damage they can cause.

This is relevant for us in the fact that we have to choose the foundation for our lives. No matter what age or stage of life you're in, the storms will come and find you. We all go through times of heartache, disappointment, sickness, breakup, failure, stress. The list can go on and on, no one is exempt, not even the wealthiest person on earth. What matters is not what you go through but how you allow it to affect you.

It may seem easier to do things our own way rather than making Jesus the Lord of our life and choosing to surrender and do things His way. While we may all like to be our own boss, after you've tried this for a while you will find that Jesus is the only Rock who can give you stability through the issues of life and He really does know best. He will lead and guide you in His ways if you give Him the opportunity.

Take a moment to think …

What storms are you going through right now? They may be physical storms going on around you or you may be experiencing some inner turmoil.

Do you need Jesus' help to come and bring some calm and stability to your life? He promises to give you peace that is so deep, it will be greater than your understanding.

ACTION STEP

Spend a few minutes in prayer. Repent for having chosen to do things your own way, ask Jesus to take charge and come and be Lord of your life. It doesn't matter how many times you may have done this in the past, there are no limits to Jesus' mercy and forgiveness, and He's delighted that you're coming to Him again!

Record what you've just done. Write it down so that you remember what just happened. Get ready to build the rest of your life on the ROCK!

_____

_____

_____

VERSE OF THE DAY

"Therefore whoever hears these sayings of Mine, and does them, I will liken him to a wise man who built his house on the rock."

Matthew 7:24

Chapter 2

How Do I Know What God Is Saying To Me?

The Bible tells us in the book of Genesis that when God created the world and everything in it, He made man and woman in His image. This means that He can talk and communicate just like we do.

Communication is vital in any relationship and we won't get very far without it. Think about one of your closest relationships and what would happen if you did all the talking and they did all the listening or even worse if nobody spoke or nobody listened!

If you read through more of the Bible, you'll find that it's filled with people who heard from God, but if you struggle to know what God's saying to you, you're not alone. It's something that I struggled with for many years, despite growing up in the church, until I realized that God was speaking to me all the time; I just had to learn to recognize His voice. I've included this question right at the beginning of this devotional to help you to actively hear His voice as you read through each chapter.

I remember a time in my 20s when I was receiving some prayer and counsel from a lady in the church. She would always end our time by giving me an encouraging word of what she felt that God wanted to say to me. This worked out great until the day when she asked me to receive a word from God for her. I remember sitting there in her living room with my eyes closed, feeling like the room was spinning and not sure what was supposed to happen next. Finally I explained how I was feeling and her reply to me was just to ask God quietly and wait to see what came into my heart or mind. As I did this, I heard "The joy of the Lord is my strength" go around in my mind and she confirmed that this was a verse that she needed to hear for the week ahead. You can imagine my excitement that the Almighty God, Creator of the universe, King of kings, would speak to me. You have to believe that this is the desire of His heart; we are called His children and of course He wants to talk to His kids. How else could we be in relationship together?

It's a journey where I've grown along the way. The more that I do it and give Him time to speak to me, the easier it is to hear from Him. God rarely speaks in a loud booming voice like He may have done in the Old Testament. Only a few people have heard the audible voice of God. We have to take the time to listen for His still, small voice.

Psalm 46 tells us to "Be still and know that I am God." There are so many distractions in today's world and we need to learn to put them aside and to spend some quality time with God. It's in the stillness that we hear His voice. Maybe that means putting away the cell phone for a little while or turning off the TV. It may involve discipline to start with but it will get easier the more you do it. Then there are the inner distractions; the thoughts or anxieties that flood your mind as soon as your outer world is quiet. It's even harder to ignore these but try to relax and focus on God and know that He promises to take care of all your concerns when you leave them in His hands.

It may help you to picture Jesus or God the Father in your mind, you may find it easier to have a visual as you prepare to hear what He wants to speak to you. Then all you need to do is ask God what He wants to say and wait to hear His words flowing up into your heart and mind, just like the experience that I shared above.

How do you know if it's God speaking to you and it's not just your own thoughts? There's no real guarantee but you just have to trust that your Heavenly Father loves you so much and has so much that He wants to say to you. His thoughts are much kinder, more generous and more loving than your own. He can also give you help, direction and creative ideas - remember He is full of wisdom! I remember taking credit for all my creative ideas and the revelations I had received before I realized that it had actually been God giving them to me!

Just like life itself, learning to hear God's voice is a journey of faith and if you need some help, ask someone you trust to confirm what you think God is speaking to you. Good leaders will always want to help you and see you grow.

ACTION STEP

Try this right now. Take a few minutes of quiet and ask God the following questions:

Do you love me?

_____

What do you want to say to me?

_____

What Bible verse or story do you want to encourage me with today?

_____

Start your journey by asking simple questions and try recording your answers in a journal so that you have a record of what God is speaking to you. I'm sure you'll be encouraged just like I was!

VERSE OF THE DAY

"My sheep hear my voice, and I know them, and they follow me."

John 10:27

Chapter 3

If God Is Good ... Why Do Bad Things Happen To Good People?

It seems like it's an age-old question and it makes me wonder just how long people have been asking it. Have they been asking it for centuries or is it a modern-day question, perhaps in part due to the 'happily ever after package' that's been sold to us by Hollywood? Who doesn't love a feel good movie with a happy ending? I'm right there with you too. I was sixteen when I watched 'Pretty Woman' on the big screen at the local cinema. Although I may cringe now at the storyline, I can still see Julia Roberts looking drop-dead gorgeous in that red dress, being swept off her feet by the equally handsome Richard Gere.

But let's get back to real life ... we don't all get to marry our Prince Charming and we don't all live happily ever after. Actually, we're not meant to, that's what eternity is for!

We don't always know what people are going through. Some people like to post it out all over social media so we know exactly what's going on in their lives.

11

Others of us will fight a more private battle with just a circle of trusted friends. We're all different. We have to find what works for us and realize that others may respond differently to their circumstances.

This is where we come to my story. I got to marry my Prince Charming in a beautiful wedding ceremony on a rainy July day back in England when I was in my mid 20s. As we set up home together, like most young brides I had dreamy expectations of what life would look like for us. However … I had not planned to journey through the valley of infertility. What was initially a shock to me became a long, lonely and painful walk that nearly sucked the life out of me, and in the early years I didn't respond well. If it wasn't time to settle down with children, then it certainly was time to hit the pubs and clubs, embrace the weekend party life and avoid the pain inside.

If I'm honest, I totally rejected God at this time in my life. I'd grown up in church, I tried to be good, I didn't understand why we couldn't have children when He is the Creator and Giver of life. Despite what the Bible says about God being for us, my heart felt like He was working against us.

He is the ultimate patient Father though and just like in the story of the prodigal son, He left me to get to the end of myself and there He was waiting with His arms wide open.

I'd like to say that it's been plain sailing since then but I would frequently return to those times of deep sadness and ask the question 'why' over and over again. Finally I realized (it took me a long time) that God is not going to answer that question. Instead of questioning His plans and His goodness, I had to come to the place of peace that comes from trusting Him. There's so much instability in life, putting your trust in God is the safest way to live.

If we accept the fact that we will go through hard times, we will see it's so much better to have the Lord right there with us, comforting us with His presence. His plan isn't to leave us in our brokenness but to lovingly put us back together and let His grace shine through.

I also had to transition my thoughts to focus on the blessings of what I do have instead of what I don't have. My heart is full when I think about my nephews and nieces, the now, young adults whose lives we got to be part of over the years, the number of youth retreats we got to lead and my sweet-natured Labrador, Luna, who thinks she's a child - I guess we've allowed her to think like that! But most of all, I'm thankful for the plans that my Heavenly Father has for my life, to enable us to travel and to meet so many people from many different nations, and to share with them His transforming love.

If you're going through hard times today, my heart is with you and so is the Heavenly Father. It may take some time, but whatever you're going through, choose to know that He is always good and choose to have Him walk through this life with you. Some days may be more difficult than others, just like they were for me but remember that He is always patiently waiting to pick you up and walk with you again.

ACTION STEP

If you have time today, read the story of the Prodigal Son in Luke 15 :11-32 and try to meditate on the compassion of the Heavenly Father and how much He loves His children.

Think about the situation you are facing today. Don't let it be a barrier between you and the Heavenly Father but take a few moments to ask Him to walk with you through this season. It's a prayer that you'll need to pray every day but one day you will get through to the other side and you will be able to recognize His goodness and faithfulness to you.

VERSE OF THE DAY

"I've never quit loving you and never will. Expect love, love and more love."

Jeremiah 31: 3 MSG

This is a verse that I read recently and wanted to share with you. This is God's attitude towards you and me!

Chapter 4

Does God Really Care About Me?

This is a very interesting question because the Bible talks about how much God loves us but sometimes life tries to scream at us that God doesn't care and we're left to work it all out for ourselves. I guess the real question is who do you believe, experience of life or the Bible?

Fourteen years ago, Jonathan and I arrived in Tulsa, Oklahoma. It was December 5th, 2006 and Tulsa was just on the other side of a snow storm. There we were with our lives packed into two suitcases each, not sure what the future would hold but believing that God would take care of us. For the next two and a half years we lived in a converted fellowship hall at a church and worked and trained for this church, who had told us before we committed to them, that they couldn't afford to pay us.

Sometimes I like to talk about how our American journey began because if you meet us now, you see us fourteen years later with a beautiful home, jobs, a business, two cars and Luna the Labrador, and maybe seem from the outside to be two people who've got it all together. How did we make it from there to here? One step at a time with the Lord leading us by the hand, then add into the mix a lot of faith, patience and perseverance. I can tell you from my experience that there is definitely no magic formula!

Jesus teaches in the Gospels that our Heavenly Father takes care of the sparrows, the lilies of the field and He even knows how many hairs are on our heads. The Bible also tells us in the book of Romans that "faith comes by hearing the Word of God" (10:17). This means that the more we read the Bible, listen to testimonies and worship songs, the more we grow in faith and believe that just as God takes care of others, He can do the same for us too.

I understand that sometimes it's hard to believe that God truly cares about your little life and circumstances when things are all pear-shaped. This is where you have to choose to believe what the Bible is telling you is true. Years ago, our church in England was giving away a CD called the Father's love letter. The person who compiled it had gone through all the verses of the Bible that talk about how God loves us and recorded them on a CD in the format of a personal letter from God. I went through a season of listening to this letter over and over again; my heart, mind and spirit all needed to hear how much God loved me. When I got to the point that I was absolutely convinced how much God loved me and it didn't depend on my circumstances or how I was feeling, I stopped listening to that same CD. It had been a tool for me to experience the love of the Father.

If you turn to the Psalms and read through chapter 139, you'll find this is an incredible Psalm that talks about how much God loves you, created you, knows you, looks out for you and thinks about you. Verses 17-18 talk about God's thoughts towards you being greater than the number of grains of sand on the shore. If you live near Gulf Shores, go down to the beach and try and get your head around how many grains of sand might possibly be on that one little beach … and then think of how many beaches there might be on this earth! That's how many thoughts God has towards you and they are all precious, kind and loving.

So I just want to share another story from my catalog of testimonies to show you how much God cares. During our years in Oklahoma we had a chocolate Labrador named Coco who lived with us for around six years. Yes, I know we definitely have a Labrador thing! Anyway, as our time in Oklahoma was coming to an end, we knew that we couldn't take Coco with us because we were going to South America for two months and had no idea where we would live after that. Without any satisfactory solution about a new home for Coco and very little time left in our house, I prayed to God and told Him that if He cared about the sparrows, then surely, He could take care of Coco. Don't you know that God loves to do miracles on our behalf?!

Very soon afterwards, a friend from the church contacted me and told me that Coco could be accepted on an inmate dog-training program in a prison near

Oklahoma City. Once we had checked into the program and were happy that it was suitable, we jokingly told people that Coco was off doing prison ministry! And once we arrived back in the US from South America our previous dog-sitter had found a couple who wanted to adopt a seven-year-old Labrador. Don't tell me that God isn't into the details of our lives!

I hope I've encouraged you with that last story. If you're feeling like you need to know how much God cares about you, I encourage you to head over to: www.fathersloveletter.com_You can still hear the letter that encouraged me all those years ago.

If you're faced with a situation where you need the Father's intervention like my story about Coco, tell Him and let Him work out the details for you.

ACTION STEP

Ask God what His thoughts are towards you and write them down below.

_____

_____

VERSE OF THE DAY

"How precious also are Your thoughts to me, O God! How great is the sum of them! If I should count them, they would be more in number than the sand."

Psalm 139:17-18

Chapter 5

The Power Of Forgiveness

Forgiveness is one of the tools that has really helped me in my life journey and has enabled me to help many others to find healing and freedom.

I grew up hearing about forgiveness, but I didn't really understand it until a number of years ago. I remember as a young child, saying my prayers before going to sleep at night and I knew all about repentance. I was always asking God to forgive me for what I'd done wrong (and I was a good child!), but I didn't understand the concept of forgiveness. I knew the importance of saying sorry but I'm not sure that I was taught how to forgive. However, it's right there in the Bible!

When Jesus came to earth and started his ministry, he brought lots of concepts that people had never heard before. He was basically teaching them a better way to live that would represent the values of the Kingdom of Heaven. You may have heard some of these new principles such as; loving your enemies, praying for those who persecute you, choosing mercy over judgement, that the first will be last … and the principle of forgiveness.

In Matthew 18, Jesus tells a parable of the Unforgiving Servant to illustrate the importance of forgiveness. In response to the parable, Peter asks the question about how many times we need to forgive … is it enough to forgive seven times? I think Peter must have thought that he was being generous with his response but Jesus came back with the number 70 x 7. I'm sure that most of us have tried to figure this out and even used a calculator, but what Jesus was saying was to forgive an infinite number of times; don't ever stop forgiving.

Aren't you glad though that God forgives us so infinitely, that there's no set limit and once you've reached it, He crosses you off the list? I'm glad that no matter how many times I get things wrong or slip up, He's always there, waiting to forgive me.

I want to set the record straight on what it means to forgive. Forgiveness means to let go, to walk away, in other words don't let a hurt or an offense become part of who you are. It does not mean that what was done to you was right or ok, it just deals with the hurt in your heart and will eventually allow you to move on from a person or situation.

I believe that forgiveness is supernatural, that we need God's grace in order to forgive. However, I know that in the secular world there is a realization of the importance of forgiveness and people are experiencing release just by saying aloud the words, "I forgive you." I also believe that in the spiritual realm or when we pray and forgive that we place that person in God's hands and allow Him to deal with the situation.

Forgiveness is such a powerful concept and we have seen many miracles and breakthroughs happen when people have released forgiveness. Probably the most powerful was after praying with a gentleman in Chile some years ago. He was in a desperate situation, needing heart surgery but after we prayed and he forgave various people who had hurt him, especially when he was young, he went back to the surgeon and was given a clean bill of health with no surgery needed. It was wonderful to see him jumping up and down in church on the following Sunday.

As I've seen the power of forgiveness at work, it really has become a life message that I try to live out. It's not easy, the deeper the hurt, the harder you need to work at forgiveness.

Ask God to show you if there's someone in your life that you need to forgive. Or maybe you already know who it is.

Then say out loud that you choose to forgive this person for how they treated you and then ask God to bless them. Keep forgiving them until you no longer feel the negative emotion toward them anymore.

As you're thinking about forgiveness, just be aware that there may be two others to add to your list. One is yourself; we are often hardest on ourselves for the mistakes that we make, and the other is God. Choose to forgive yourself, let yourself off the hook and know that God has already forgiven you!

Some people do struggle with the thought of forgiving God. If He is perfect, then why should we have to forgive Him? You may have noticed throughout life that God doesn't always answer your prayers the way that you wanted Him to. How did this make you feel? What you're actually doing is forgiving your perception of God and what you thought He should or shouldn't have done. For example, He allowed someone to die when you prayed for them, He didn't stop a relationship from breaking up, or plans from failing. Forgiving God for not acting in those situations will just clear your heart and allow you to have a closer relationship with Him.

ACTION STEP

If you have some time today, read the parable in Matthew 18:21-35, it will make you thankful for our Heavenly Father's forgiveness.

_____

_____

VERSE OF THE DAY

"As it turns out, forgiveness is your habit, and that is why you're worshiped."

Psalm 130:4 MSG

Everyday there are opportunities to become hurt and offended. Let's follow the example of the Lord and make forgiveness one of our daily habits!

Chapter 6

Take Care Of Your Heart

When it comes to physical or emotional health, the heart is at the very core of our being and taking care of it should be our number one priority!

A few years ago when I moved down to the Gulf Coast from Oklahoma and started working at the Full Armor Center with Dr. Alicia, I started to learn a lot more about health and wellness and just like many things, I had to go back to basics. I learned about the importance of gut health. If your gut isn't healthy, it doesn't matter how many supplements and healthy foods you consume, your body won't be able to absorb the nutrition correctly.

It's the same with the heart, if your heart isn't healthy from a spiritual point of view, it doesn't matter how much time you spend reading the Bible or in your prayer closet, your heart isn't going to absorb the nourishment of the Word.

This is what the book of Proverbs says about your heart:

"Guard your heart with all diligence for out of it spring the issues of life." Proverbs 4:23

When the Bible talks about the heart, it has a much broader meaning than what we're used to. It means the mind, will and emotions; it's our inner man or woman and the essence of who we are. It is central to our very being and we need to spend time taking care of it. The Bible tells us that even though we may concentrate on our outer appearance, God is more interested in the heart and that's why he chose the young shepherd boy David over all his older brothers, to be the greatest king of Israel.

When was the last time you took a quick peek at what was going on in your heart? It's so important to check on our spiritual health. Oftentimes we need to ask God to come and help us, just like David did in Psalms 51, where he asked God to search his heart and find any wickedness that might be in there.

There could be someone you've not forgiven, maybe some jealousy, anger, lustful thoughts or pride … none of us is perfect. It's all about the Holy Spirit shining His light into our hearts, bringing His healing and making us more like Christ day by day. If you're still not sure what's in your heart, listen to your words: "for out of the abundance of the heart, his mouth speaks", is what it says in Luke 6:45. In other words, if it's in your heart, it will eventually come out of your mouth!

I can recall a situation where someone had taken advantage of us, had ended up squatting in the house we had in England and put us in a very difficult and uncomfortable position. While I was doing my best to forgive this lady, because I knew that this was what I needed to do, I had a dream one night where I saw her and out of my own mouth came the words, "I hate you." I had no idea that there was hate in my heart, but the Lord did, He wanted to reveal it to me so that I could deal with it. So, I asked one of my mentors to pray with me and the Lord helped me to clean up this area of my heart. I'm so thankful that the Holy Spirit helps us to deal with the issues of our hearts.

So, what does it mean to guard or protect your heart? It may mean the opposite of what you thought it did. It doesn't mean to build a huge wall around it so that no one can get close to you. God designed us for relationship with Him and each other and that's why we need to keep it soft. The best way to do this is to spend time in His presence and tell Him honestly what's going on and how you feel about it. Don't even worry if your words and emotions get a little colorful; He already knows, and you won't make Him blush! He does like to hear from you though and I sometimes like to journal out my thoughts. I write honestly how I'm feeling and wait to hear what He wants to speak to me.

ACTION STEP

I'd like to encourage you now to take a few moments to look into your heart and ask God to heal you where you've been hurt and forgive you where you've been wrong. You may also need to forgive those who've hurt you.

_____

_____

Remember that God is always with you, He promised to never leave you. Ask Him to help you to guard your heart as you walk through life with His wisdom.

VERSE OF THE DAY

"For the Lord does not see as man sees; for man looks at the outward appearance, but the Lord looks at the heart."

1 Sam 16:7

Chapter 7

Free To Be You

D id you know that you are absolutely unique and that there is no one who is exactly the same as you on the whole planet? I even have identical twin nieces in my family and when they were young and dressed in the same outfits, it was difficult to tell them apart but then their personalities would shine through and that happened more as they got older.

Think of yourself as a masterpiece that's all the more valuable because you're unique. You may not think of yourself like this especially if you're still in the lockdown / quarantine slump, wearing comfy pants and ponytails … I think we've all been there in 2020/21. But it's right there in the Bible in Ephesians 2:10, "For we are His workmanship, created in Christ Jesus." We are hand-crafted and lovingly put together by the Master Designer who never makes a mistake! Now doesn't that make you feel better about yourself?

That's the kind of truth that you need to think about because there are so many subliminal messages telling you that you're not enough. Even in the church there can be a lie that you start to believe, usually that you have to be perfect or just be like everyone else, in order to fit in or in order to serve. Let me tell you how it affected me.

I have to take you back nearly thirty years (and I don't know how the time possibly flew by so fast), but I'm going back to my first mission trip at twenty years old. I went with Operation Mobilization on their Love Europe campaign, which consisted of one-week training in Germany and three weeks on the mission field in a different country, which for me was Morocco. There were several thousand young people at the training, and I can remember feeling overwhelmed, alone, because I had gone there by myself, and felt I didn't fit in. What use would I be to the mission team when I was quiet and shy and who they really needed on the team were the loud, talkative evangelists! These were my own thoughts but one day, one of the older Irish girls told me how much I had blessed her by my gentle spirit. Up until this point I hadn't valued the gift of gentleness, but God used this girl to speak into my life to help me to value the person He had made me.

I've learned a lot and come a long way since this point. I know that God loves to use all sorts of characters in His evangelistic army and when we value the gift that He has put inside of us, He will use it for His glory! On the other hand, of course, the Devil knows how powerful we can be when we're living out who God has created us to be and that's why he tries so hard to convince us to become someone we're never meant to be.

Of course, I'm no longer so shy and quiet. I've grown in confidence and I'm never sure if God designed me as an introvert or an extrovert, maybe the perfect mix of both. Like most of us, I've traveled along the road of learning to love myself. If you can't love yourself, you can't love others, it's plain to see in the greatest commandment which says:

"'Love the Lord your God with all your heart and with all your soul and with all your mind.' This is the first and great commandment. And the second is like it: 'Love your neighbor as yourself.'" (Matthew 22:37-39)

For some reason we seem to see our flaws, whether they are physical or in our character, under a magnifying glass and we don't allow ourselves to appreciate our assets. As I've grown older, I've come to peace with my physical appearance, it doesn't mean that I've stopped working at it but I don't take myself so seriously anymore. You don't have to live the perfect life that only exists through photoshop on social media, you just have to live the life that God has designed for you and become the person He created you to be.

ACTION STEP

Meditate on this verse and let the truth of it settle into your spirit. Ask God to give you the strength to start overlooking some of your flaws and ask Him to show you the things He loves about you. Make sure you write down what He tells you below:

_____

_____

If you've always found it hard to love and accept yourself, concentrate on how much God loves you and is crazy about you and you will naturally start to love yourself more.

VERSE OF THE DAY

"You are altogether beautiful, my darling; there is no flaw in you."

Song of Solomon 4:7 NIV

Chapter 8

How Do I Know God's Will For My Life?

Just recently one of my nieces asked me about a decision that she needed to make. She was about to embark on a new career path and had to choose between three options (lucky girl)! It wasn't my job to make the decision for her, I simply asked her questions to help her find out what was in her heart. Let's be certain though, if I did have some big concerns, I would have told her.

Making decisions can be difficult and we don't want to get it wrong. Maybe this is where we have to move away from the image in our heads that Father God is up in the heavens, just waiting for us to make a wrong move and that's when He'll get out His big stick. Maybe you don't even want to ask God to help you make a decision because you're afraid that He won't let you do what you want to do. I've been there too.

So let's get this straight, the Bible says that He knows the plans that He has for us, plans to prosper and not to harm us, to give us hope and a future (Jeremiah 29:11).

They sound like good plans to me! He also wants us to have the best life ever; we just have to navigate through it.

You may not have realized this yet, but God gives us lots of freedom to make our own decisions and even when we get it wrong, He still loves us unconditionally. A number of years ago our Pastor shared with us about the wise men who went to Bethlehem to visit the infant Jesus. They followed a star and then searched out the baby. The meaning of that word 'searched' tells us that they looked for Him by trial and error. They didn't find Him right away. Their first stop was the Palace, which may have seemed like a logical place, but it actually put Jesus' life in danger because Herod wanted to kill the baby when he found out about Him. You could say that they got it wrong, but God is so much bigger than our mistakes, and just like the wisemen, we shake it off and get on with our journey.

During 2016 we were making the decision to move from Oklahoma to Alabama. After our Pastor had shared with us his vision to move to the Gulf Coast to start a church here, and had invited the leadership of the current church to consider coming to help, the first thing we did was to plan a visit. If you're planning to move to a new place, you definitely need to go and check it out first.

In the Old Testament there's a story about the Israelites going to spy out the Promised Land. God had promised the people a land that was rich and fertile, flowing with milk and honey but He told them that they needed to go and take possession of it. Moses was the leader of Israel at the time and he sent in twelve spies to see what the land was like. You may know that only Joshua and Caleb saw the possibilities of the land while the other ten spies were afraid of what they saw in the land. Because they didn't believe they could take it, the sad end of their story is that they ended up wandering in the wilderness for 40 years.

It's definitely a story that we can learn from and the principle is there: to check out the land. The first time we came to visit Foley we knew that it was a place we could call home but there were still some giants to slay before that would happen. Selling our home and then leaving our friends and spiritual family in Oklahoma to move 800 miles away to a place where we barely knew anyone, where we would have to find new jobs, a new home and start another business. At the time, it may have been easier to stay in the safe place where we were but we had the conviction in our hearts that this was the right thing to do, and that's what propelled us forward.

I remember at one point Jonathan asked me, "What if it doesn't work out?" My response to him was that we'd have to move back to England, which would not be an easy task either. However, we partnered our faith with God's vision and as we took each step, He started to work things out for us.

I have to say it wasn't a quick decision and we didn't make it on our own. We shared our plans with our families, my parents even accompanied us on our first trip. In addition, we prayed with friends who we consider to be spiritual advisors. We were in good health to be able to make the move, we had the finances to do it and most importantly we had the desire to move and the peace in our hearts that this was the right step for us. The rest is history!

If you're facing a decision, be sure to only move forward with peace in your heart. Don't make the mistake of just doing your own thing and asking God to bless it, as this way will take you longer to get where you actually want to go. But don't be so afraid of getting it wrong that you just stay where you are.

ACTION STEP

Look back on your life and think of a time when you were facing a big decision. How did you come to that decision and was it the right or wrong thing to do? Then think about how you would make a big decision now.

VERSE OF THE DAY

"Trust in the Lord and do good; dwell in the land and enjoy safe pasture. Take delight in the Lord, and He will give you the desires of your heart."

Psalm 37:3-4 NIV

Chapter 9

Just Do It!

Is there something that you'd love to do or to try, but for some reason or another you just don't get around to doing it? Have you ever thought about what holds you bac?

You may tell yourself that you don't have time, or money but sometimes it may be a case of just setting priorities. Then there is FEAR! The fear of doing something new … and maybe not getting it right. Perfectionism is a killer. If You fall victim to it, it will rob you of enjoying some of life's best experiences.

One piece of advice that I was given as I was just starting out on the path towards ministry was very simple; "You have to knock for the door to be opened." I've thought back on these words at different points in my life and found them to be so true. We live in a world where we seem to be surrounded by YouTube or Instagram overnight sensations and maybe live with the vague hope that one day it will happen to us! The reality is though that we don't see all the hard work and practice behind the scenes, and we can't spend all our time 'waiting' for opportunity to knock at the door. Take the bull by the horns and do it!

Surround yourself with people who inspire you, encourage you and cause you to grow. There's a verse in Proverbs 27 which says: "As iron sharpens iron, so one person sharpens another," (v. 17). Just recently I've been inspired by my husband, Jonathan, who started playing the piano, and also by a friend who started a Christian newspaper, and another friend who has started a nonprofit organization to help in the fight against human trafficking. I had it in my heart to write this devotional for a number of years before I started putting pen to paper so to speak. I didn't have any excuse, any writer's block, I just needed to get down and do it. It was the example of these three people that motivated me to get going!

The Bible is full of true stories that are meant to inspire us. So many ordinary people who obeyed God and accomplished BIG things for His Kingdom. One of those amazing stories is Peter, who got out of the boat and walked on the water.

The story takes place on Lake Galilee. It's a familiar place for the disciples, many of whom are seasoned fishermen. As it's getting dark, Jesus sends them out to cross to the other side of the lake, while he stays behind to pray. All of a sudden, a storm starts to brew, and they are already far away from shore. In the darkness the wind and the waves are thrashing against the boat and these brave fishermen are terrified. Then along comes Jesus, walking on the water and appearing like a ghost. If I had been in that situation and Jesus came to rescue me, I would just have said to him, "Lord, get me out of here!" But Peter has a different reaction. He sees Jesus walking on the water, faith starts to rise in him, and he wants to see that same miracle manifest in him. Peter calls out to Jesus and says, "Lord, if it is you, command me to come to you on the water," (Matthew 14 :28). Peter had to take that first step out of the boat into the unknown, and miraculously he walked on the water, just like Jesus! Imagine what that experience was like for Peter. He accomplished something that is physically impossible.

If you're familiar with the story, you know that when Peter took his eyes off Jesus and looked at the scariness of the waves, he started to sink. That's an important principle to follow, whatever you're going through, keep your eyes on Jesus and His presence and not the storm of life that's surrounding you.

God wants you to live the best life possible. There were eleven other disciples in the boat but only one took that leap of faith and got to walk on the water. Even when Peter started to sink, he got to experience what it was like to be caught by Jesus, as He reached out his hand, pulled him out of the water and helped him into the boat.

We're all called to live out our own adventure. I love to travel but I'm not your regular tourist. I like to go off the beaten tourist path. In 2016 when Jonathan and I went to South America for two months, we took some time to visit Machu Picchu in Peru. It is not an easy place to get to. If I remember correctly, it took numerous flights, two trains, two buses and some hiking to get there. It took time, effort, energy and money but the reward was worth it. I still remember on our day there, Jonathan going on slightly ahead of me and as he rounded the corner, I heard him gasp. The site was soooooo breathtaking. It has definitely been one of the best experiences of my life so far.

2020/21 has not been a time for so many physical adventures. There seems to be so much uncertainty in the world; but cling on to God, just like Peter did. He's the same yesterday, today and forever and He will still take you on an adventure with Him.

We've talked about dreams and about God's will for your life. Maybe there's something that you're wanting to do? Move to a new city, go back to school, learn a language, take up a new sport, musical instrument or hobby? How about starting your own business? I'm not telling you to make a reckless decision but allow God to lead you into new adventures.

ACTION STEP

Be sure to read the story of Peter in Matthew 14:22-33. It may inspire you to take a step out of the boat, and you'll probably find that you weren't that comfortable there anyway.

_____

_____

QUOTE OF THE DAY

"Life is either a daring adventure or nothing at all."

Helen Keller (1880-1968),
American author and educator,
known for her courage
in the face of overwhelming odds.

Chapter 10

What Are The Voices In Your Head Telling You?

No, I'm not talking about zombies or anything weird but have you ever had a silent conversation with yourself? I'm mentioning this because I recently went back to working out after a long Covid-related absence; not that I was sick, just taking a break from the gym environment. There I was in this session deciding how many rounds and reps I was going to do but as I was working through it and it got more difficult, I was trying to convince myself that I'd done enough and it was ok to quit. Then my stubborn, determined side kicked in and told my flesh that I was going to push on through. Somehow, I got it done!

Whether you know it or not, a lot of our strength is in the mind and our actions are determined by our thoughts. The Bible tells us in Proverbs 23:7 that "as a man thinks in his heart, so he is." We are basically shaped by our thoughts and that's why it's so important to think about what we're thinking about.

Nowadays we have lots of tools to help to get our thoughts on the right path. Just pop into Hobby Lobby or go on to Instagram and you can find lots of motivational quotes to get you through the day. I'm surrounded by quotes at work and right by my desk I have one that says, "Not all stars belong to the sky". That's my motivation to shine my light a little brighter. Do you have your own motto that helps you get through life?

A motto, mantra or life quote can be for a season and you may need to adopt a new one for a new situation. A number of years ago, I was living in Oklahoma and working a part-time job that was rarely rewarding. Often, I would come home and write off what had been another bad day, until the Lord challenged me on this. I happened to be reading a devotional in which the writer said that as Christians, we don't have the luxury to have bad days. He quoted Ephesians 1:3 which says that we have been blessed with every spiritual blessing.

This really struck a chord with me, especially because he was in a far-off nation where believers know what it really is to suffer. Here I was simply not enjoying my days and something had to change. So, I created a motto and started to tell myself that "every day is a great day in the kingdom" (of God, that is). I had a small chalk board at home, so I wrote it on there too and read it out loud before I started my day. It was just a small step and things didn't change right away but after a while I noticed that I was happier, my joy had increased, and I became a more joyful person. Nothing had changed in my circumstances, but my thoughts and my attitude had changed.

It's been five or so years since that time and I don't need to tell myself this motto anymore. I've trained myself to expect a great day every day because God is with me and will take care of me, whatever else happens. I maybe don't have a life quote that I need right now but I try to fill my mind with lots of good Bible verses to meditate on.

Philippians 4:8 says: "Finally, brothers and sisters, whatever is true, whatever is noble, whatever is right, whatever is pure, whatever is lovely, whatever is admirable—if anything is excellent or praiseworthy— think about such things." NIV

In a world of negativity, this is such wise instruction. It's not always easy and it requires discipline. I've had times where I've felt my thoughts wandering in a negative direction and I've literally imagined myself grabbing hold of them and dragging them back to think good, pure and lovely thoughts.

Remember that our thoughts become our words, actions and attitudes and we have the ability to affect the atmosphere around us. Think big and think positive, but most of all make sure that your thoughts are in line with what the Bible says.

If you recognize that your thoughts have been more negative than positive, determine in your heart to change and focus on the verse above from Philippians, which is our verse of the day.

ACTION STEP

Write down what change you want to see in your life by changing your thoughts. For example, I started to have more joy in my life and my days were happier. What do you want to see? In 6 to 12 months you should look back at this and see what a difference it has made.

_____

_____

QUOTE OF THE DAY

My life quote will always be: "Every day is a great day in the Kingdom."

Write down a quote that inspires you during this season of life. If you don't have one, ask God to give you one.

_____

_____

Chapter 11

Hang On To Your Hope

Today's verse of the day is from the book of Jeremiah. It talks about the hope God has for our lives because He knows the plans for our future. This word came at a time in Israel's history when they were just about to be taken into captivity, but God was telling them that this wasn't the end of the story. I'm sure that the Israelites and countless people since then have held on to this verse to get them through difficult times.

I know that I have walked through a very dark period of my life when it was difficult to hold on to hope and I wasn't sure that I wanted to go on, but looking back now, I am so thankful that my Heavenly Father gave me enough strength to keep going. When I think about the life I have led and how many other lives I have touched since that time, I know it's only because of His grace and His amazing love for me.

However, unlike my story, there are many people who don't manage to keep going forward. Every day there is a report or a prayer request for someone who has given up and taken their own life just to end their pain and suffering. Suicide used to be associated with drug induced death but now it's people living alongside us who take that decision to end it all.

To be honest no one knows 100% what happens to people who commit suicide. I remember discussions about suicide being the unforgivable sin, but I simply choose to believe that God is merciful and will reach out and save people at the very last minute. What we do know is that suicide has a devastating effect on the family who are left to pick up the pieces and walk through the grief, blame, guilt, questions and doubts. This is why we are called to be a source of hope to our communities.

With today's pandemic it's a good idea to be more aware of those around us. Many more people are suffering from loneliness than ever before. Look out for those experiencing loneliness and reach out to them however you can, even a text to tell someone you're thinking about them and praying for them can make a big difference to someone's day.

How about you? How are you doing? We live in such a stressed-out world that it's difficult to know what's normal behavior anymore. Thankfully we have technology to help us. Jonathan has an Apple Watch that will ding and remind him to breathe. You have to breathe through those stressful times. I have an Oura Ring that tells me if I need to have a rest day and take it easy and other days, I need to be more active! So, these are tools that can definitely help us out.

If you're going through a tough time though, I want to encourage you to keep on going. It was Winston Churchill who said, "If you're going through hell, keep on going." He should know, he led a nation from defeat to victory. King David wrote in Psalms 23:4 (KJV) "Yea, though I walk through the valley of the shadow of death, I will fear no evil." He knew about those dark times too. Most of us will go through them at some point in our lives, but they are usually just for a season and not forever.

When you're going through a dark time, one temptation is to isolate yourself, but you need to do the opposite and find someone safe who you can open up to. Don't look around you and think that everyone else has a perfect life with absolutely no issues; that's simply not true. Just find a friend who won't judge you and will let you be real with them.

Our thoughts can definitely get us into trouble, don't let them lead you down a dark path. I realized at a certain point that it wasn't always my circumstances that were bringing me down, it was just my thoughts. This was when I needed to bring back my wandering thoughts and stand on the truth of God's Word.

What does God say about you? He loves you, you are valuable to Him, only you can fulfill the purpose that He has for you, no one else can touch other people's lives in just the way that you can. Ask God how He feels about you or find some verses that talk about His love for YOU, write them down and exchange your own thoughts for God's thoughts.

God is always there no matter how desperate things may seem. The band, Third Day, has a song called 'Cry out to Jesus'. I was at one of their concerts when I heard them tell the story behind the song. One night a young man went out in his car to commit suicide, and then decided to listen to the radio one more time before taking his life. It was this song by Third Day that was playing, the young man cried out to Jesus who heard him and saved his life that night. Jesus is always there, He is a friend who is closer than a brother. He will walk with you every day, don't think that you have to wait until things are desperate to cry out to Him. He promises to do life with you.

ACTION STEP

Write down some of the promises from the Bible that encourage you to keep going through difficult times and to have hope. Be sure to change some of your negative thoughts to these truths.

_____

_____

VERSE OF THE DAY

"For I know the plans I have for you," declares the LORD, "plans to prosper you and not to harm you, plans to give you hope and a future."

Jeremiah 29:11 NIV

Chapter 12

What's Keeping You Up At Night?

Maybe you've found that your worst fears come out at night, maybe like ghosts hiding in the closet? You may read this and think, 'Oh, be serious now!' But I can honestly tell you that this is what happened to me.

Let's back up a little bit. I know we all have fears, but I would never have described myself as a fearful person. Then I happened to find myself in a place where my fears were coming to the surface, and in my mind, there were some ghosts or something in the closet.

It all came to a head when someone close to me passed away, and that event happened when I was away from home. When I came back home, it was to an empty house because Jonathan was also away on a trip. The first thing I did at home was to turn on lots of lights because it was nighttime, and also to check all the closets. Those close to me who I've shared this story with, asked me what I expected to find in the closets, and I don't really know, I just needed to know that they were clear. Checking closets when I've stayed on my own in hotel rooms is something

I've done for years and I've never thought it was strange behavior. However, that night as I experienced some paralyzing fears, I knew that something was wrong.

You see we're often not aware of what's in our hearts, but God will use every situation for His and our own good, if we let Him. Despite being full of faith and adventure, there was still part of my heart that was locked in fear, and God wanted to bring freedom to that area.

What did I do after I got through that night? I didn't want to go through another one like that so I called my Pastor's wife, my good friend, Tondi, and together we found out where those fears had come from. In my case, they were from the house I grew up in, which to a young girl could have appeared cold and dark, with some unexplained noises.

Do I still have the same fears? I'm not entirely sure because I've not spent a night on my own since then. But now that I've received healing from these memories, the 'Jesus in me' can stand up to any spirit of fear that threatens to intimidate me, and I don't have to be fearful anymore.

There's a verse in the New Testament, in 2 Timothy 1:7 which says: "For God has not given us a spirit of fear but of power, love and a sound mind." Often those irrational fears lurk around in our minds, but we need the healing in the heart to take out the root of where they came from, and then we can take authority over them with our mind.

Like me you may not be aware of some of your fears or you may already consider yourself a fearful person. God knows that we all struggle with fear. The verse above was Apostle Paul's encouragement to his younger disciple Timothy, who was a pastor. In the Old Testament God commanded Joshua, the leader of Israel, not to fear but to be strong and courageous. No matter who we are, it seems that in startling situations our human reaction is to feel fear, but God wants us to trust Him. I've heard it said that the three little words 'Do Not Fear', have been written 365 times in the Bible, that's one for every day of the year!

When the pandemic hit in 2020 and the world experienced something it has not seen before, I'm sure that the whole situation caused many people's fears to surface. Fear of the future, fear of getting sick, fear of losing income and not being able to feed the family, fear of being alone and maybe most significantly the fear that comes from the unknown, not knowing what's going to happen next.

The Bible offers so many words of comfort when we find ourselves in these situations faced with our fears. Whatever life is throwing at you, God doesn't want you to live in fear, He wants you to live that abundant life that He has planned for you.

As we were coming to the end of that year, I heard the presenters on my favorite radio show announce the most searched verse of the year (on the Bible App) and this is what it was: "So do not fear, for I am with you; do not be dismayed, for I am your God. I will strengthen you and help you; I will uphold you with my righteous right hand." Isaiah 41:10 NIV

The Bible contains a wealth of comforting, empowering verses that you can anchor yourself to in fearful times. Remember you are not bound by your fear. I know I've heard it described as "False Evidence Appearing Real', so you can subject that fear to some truth from God's word.

ACTION STEP

Ask God to reveal where any of your fears have come from and then ask Him to bring His healing to those areas.

_____

_____

Move forward in the knowledge that your confidence comes from knowing that God is with you and there's nothing that you're going to have to face that you can't handle together.

VERSE OF THE DAY

How can I choose anything other than the verse of the year for 2020?

"So do not fear, for I am with you; do not be dismayed, for I am your God. I will strengthen you and help you; I will uphold you with my righteous right hand."

Isaiah 41:10

Chapter 13

What Dream Has the Father Put In Your Heart?

You may have to dig deep to answer this question and it may have been a while since you believed you could dream, before life and probably some of its disappointments got in the way. Maybe you don't even remember what dreams lie deep within your heart, but our Heavenly Father wants to help you to bring them back to life. He created you to dream. Big Dreams! The Bible says that He is able to do more than we can possibly ask or imagine and that's something that I've definitely seen in my life.

When I went to University in England at age eighteen my intention was to study French with Economics, both subjects that I loved. To cut a long story short, I ended up studying French with Spanish and I'll be honest and say that I didn't really want to study the Spanish. Well I got more than I bargained for. At the same time as studying the language I began to learn about Latin America, her people, culture and the problems she faced. My teacher was from Chile and as she started to share experiences with us, a small fire started to kindle in my heart. I wanted to go to Latin America, and most importantly to Chile.

There were different steps I could have taken to make my dream become a reality but in some ways, I took an opposite path. I graduated from University, took a permanent job and made plans to get married. At one point I even turned down an offer to go to Chile with a friend. Going to Latin American was becoming a more distant and unachievable dream!

However, In 2007 I made my first trip to Chile, fifteen years after I first dreamed of going there and I've been there fifteen times now in total. We've taken teams, led youth retreats, ministered in different churches and above all we got connected with the Chilean people, some of whom have become important members of our spiritual family.

I'm sure I had reached a point where I felt that this dream wasn't going to happen, and I placed it on the shelf to gather dust. It was after attending a School of Ministry in Toronto and then connecting with a church in Oklahoma that was planting a church in Santiago, Chile, that my dream started to take shape. You see God knows exactly where you are, where you need to be and how to get you to the place of living out your destiny.

This kind of dream doesn't happen overnight, there may be many struggles to get through until it starts to become reality. There's a story in the Bible that illustrates how true this is. Do you remember Joseph in the Old

Testament? Maybe you've seen the movie or the musical, with his technicolor dreamcoat!

As a young boy growing up with his brothers, God gave him some extraordinary dreams, but before they became true, life seemed to get harder and harder for him. Maybe Joseph should have kept his dreams to himself instead of almost 'boasting' to his brothers, that one day they would all bow down to him, because this made them hate him more than they did already, so much so that they sold him off as a slave. They must have really hated their brother to sell him and send him to Egypt!

As Joseph arrived in Egypt things initially went well for him even as a slave, he found favor with his master. Until one day his master's wife falsely accused him of making sexual advances and Joseph was thrown into jail. At this point life must have seemed exceedingly bleak for Joseph but even in deep despair he remained faithful to God and to the dreams that were in his heart. Even though it looked like so many people were against Joseph and his situation was hopeless, through a series of events, God used Joseph's path to lead him to his destiny as a deliverer for the Israelites. One day his family would all come and bow down before him just like he had seen in the dream. His story is found in Genesis, chapters 37-47. It's quite a long story but one that's definitely worth reading to show how God can bring out good in any situation.

Dreams are so important, whether it's something that God shows you while you're sleeping or the desires that you have in your heart. Dreams allow us to believe in greater or maybe impossible things and not to settle for second best. No matter where you are in life, God has His best for you!

Take a moment and ask God to show you what dreams He's placed in your heart. You may need to ask Him to revive them again. Maybe like me you've seen certain dreams come to pass and it's time to ask Him to put new dreams in your heart. He has called you to be a dreamer, to partner with Him and to start seeing miracles happen all around you.

ACTION STEP

If you're feeling a little bit like Joseph, that you're just hanging on to the dream with all you have, ask God to give you His grace while you're waiting and to trust Him to bring it into being, in His timing.

Write down a dream you have in the space below, then pray and commit it into God's hands:

_____

_____

VERSE OF THE DAY

"Now all glory to God, who is able, through his mighty power at work within us, to accomplish infinitely more than we might ask or think."

Ephesians 3:20 NLT

Dream big, daring and adventurous dreams. Remember if it's not big enough it's not God's dream for you!

Chapter 14

Use It Or Lose It!

I'm sure you've heard someone say that "you never forget how to ride a bicycle". I think it's probably true because I haven't ridden much since childhood, but I can still ride without a problem, although I may have lost some of my road confidence! However, there are other skills that you may have acquired that you need to use regularly, or you'll lose them.

Just ask me ... I spent years at school and then university studying French and perfecting my skills to sound as authentically French as possible. Now, many years later living in Southern Alabama, I have very few opportunities to practice my language skills. Speaking French is pretty far removed from my daily life here, in fact there are probably people in my inner circle who don't even know that I speak fluent French.

How about something that may be easier to identify with? What about working out and growing muscle? It's something that most of us try at least once during our lives. I surprised even myself by doing CrossFit for a couple of years when I first moved to the area. I was even more surprised by how much I loved it and the buzz of lifting heavier weights, weights that I would never have considered myself ever being able to lift! Then my season of CrossFitting came to an end and even though I still work out, I can't lift those same heavy weights anymore. The principle is the same: use the muscle or lose the muscle!

Jesus tells a story in the Gospel of Matthew to illustrate how we've all been given different talents, and how it's our responsibility to use them for His kingdom. I used to dislike this parable and it even made me fearful because I felt like I was the third servant in the story who only had one talent compared to the other two servants who had more talents than him. This servant hid his talent in the ground because he was afraid of the master. Maybe he was afraid of losing it or even afraid that he didn't have any abilities. He had given up before he even started anything.

At one point I felt the same way, that I didn't have many abilities and I was probably so fearful because I felt like I wasn't doing anything. One day as I was starting to get a fresh revelation of who God really is and His great love, He opened my eyes to start seeing myself as He saw me. He is a loving Father who celebrates our successes (big and small) and is more interested in what we are doing and who we are becoming, instead of criticizing what we're not doing. He's made me realize over time that He makes us all unique with our own gifts and talents. No one can bring joy to the Heavenly Father just like you can!

We also have an enemy who knows how powerful we will be once we fully know who we are and what talents we can use for the Kingdom. Of course he wants you to bury your talents but God wants you to grow into the person He created you to be.

What's exciting is that once you start using your talents, He gives you more and more!

Ask God to show you what talents He's given to you. If you're not sure, think about what you already enjoy doing. Do you like giving gifts to people? Do you enjoy cooking, or playing sports or playing a musical instrument?

_____

Ask God to give you ideas on how to use your gifts to bless other people.

_____

_____

Just to illustrate my last point, let me tell you a little story about Jonathan. When I first met Jonathan, he used to play the bass guitar. He could play it well, mind you, he could put some funk into the bass line! He played it faithfully for many years and one day he decided to take up the guitar. Now he's singing, leading worship and learning to play the keys.

Sorry to brag, but it illustrates my point of the multiplication of the talents. Of course, it involves work too, but God will always bless the work of our hands.

ACTION STEP

If you have time today, read the whole parable in Matthew 25:14-29.

_____

_____

VERSE OF THE DAY

"To those who use well what they are given, even more will be given, and they will have it in abundance."

Matthew 25:29 NLT

Chapter 15

Don't Miss Your Destiny

I don't want you to read this and panic and maybe even think that you might have missed it already. What I know about our Heavenly Father is that He is super merciful, every day is a fresh start with Him, and He gives us billions of chances to get things right. However, this last thought has to be balanced with the fact that Jesus paid the ultimate sacrifice for us to be able to have a relationship with the Father and to walk in the destiny that He has for us.

If you look at the worldview of destiny, it kind of equates to some invisible force like fate that will eventually lead you to where you're supposed to be. The Bible tells us that God has a pre-ordained path for your life but it does require your cooperation and faith to walk along it. With this in mind, I want to illustrate how our choices can affect our outcome.

We make choices all the time, oftentimes it's what's best for us in the moment. There's a story in the book of Genesis where a choice is made in the moment without any regard to the consequences. It's the story of twin brothers, Jacob and Esau. Esau was the first born who was a skilled hunter and his father's favorite while Jacob was a peaceful man who was favored by his mother.

The story goes that Esau has been out in the field all day, he comes back home and he's weary and hungry. As luck has it, Jacob is cooking a big pot of stew and it smells so good. Can you imagine the scene right now? Weariness is something that affects us all and comfort food is something that can make us feel so much better.

At this point the story becomes a little strange for the modern reader. Jacob tells Esau that he will give him some stew, only if Esau will sell his birthright to him. Talk about being opportunistic! However, it doesn't worry Esau, who says: "I'm about to die, so what is this birthright to me?" (Genesis 25:32). A little bit dramatic but Esau swore to Jacob that he was selling his birthright to him, which means that he completely bound himself to fulfill this oath to his brother. It says he arose, ate, drank and went on his way, normal things that we do every day but Esau had no idea what he was doing, he was so focused on how he was feeling in the moment.

The act of receiving a blessing from a father when he was about to die was very important in Old Testament culture and when Esau realized fully what he had done, he was devastated … but it was too late. It's a story of trickery and deception but ultimately God's plans are worked out in the midst of it all.

It may seem all very insignificant, but Esau is mentioned in the New Testament by the writer of the book of Hebrews, who warns us not to be a godless person like Esau, who despised his birthright. He gave up an extra share of property and wealth, his position as head of the family and most importantly the blessing he would have received, which came down from Abraham, which would have placed him in close and favored, covenant relationship with God. Here we have it…. Esau did not value his relationship with God, he gave it up for a bowl of stew!

So that was Esau's sorry story, but do you ever find yourself in his position? Remember we said that he was weary. Take a moment to think about what makes you weary, you can also use a word that's more relevant to you … burned out, stressed, exhausted, overtired, spent. What happens to you when you get like that?

Let's be honest, weariness gets to us all. With me it certainly makes life harder to handle, it's more difficult to be joyful and my words may be sharper instead of sweet. But it might not stop there, it may be an extra drink, spending some extra money or forming a relationship that feels good at the time.

I want to look again at what Esau said because it's so important:

"Look I am about to die, so what is this birthright to me?" What he was saying was, what good is that going to be to me in the future, when this is how I feel right now?

Sometimes we need to push past the feelings of the down days and negative talk and remember that God has a destiny for us, if we will keep cooperating with Him and walking along the path He has for our lives. If you're wondering whether this Christian life is all worth it and where are all the blessings mentioned in the Bible, I want to encourage you to steady your heart, focus on Jesus and His amazing love and keep pushing through the difficult times. Jesus Himself knows that there are no shortcuts to your destiny.

ACTION STEP

Determine to value your relationship with God over everything else. Sometimes this will be a daily choice but the long-term blessings will be worth it!

Write the destiny you are believing for in the space below:

_____

_____

VERSE OF THE DAY

"Watch out for the Esau syndrome: trading away God's lifelong gift in order to satisfy a short-term appetite. You well know how Esau later regretted that impulsive act and wanted God's blessing—but by then it was too late, tears or no tears."

Hebrews 12:16-17 MSG

Chapter 16

Is Your Heart In Lockdown?

I'm not sure when you'll be reading this but in 2020 'lockdown' was the word of the year. It pretty much describes how we had to live with six feet between you and the next person in order to be socially distanced. For some it was incredibly difficult and lonely without physical contact with loved ones and for others of us, we may have enjoyed a break from those crazy huggers who like to launch into our personal space. So you may have guessed which camp I'm in! If you're now thinking that I'm a fake hugger, I can just say that I've learned to hug and I realize it's an important way of expressing God's love to others, but I'm definitely not against taking a break now and then!

This being said, it's not easy to function at our full capacity when we're physically isolated. God didn't design us like that, but many of us can find ourselves living life surrounded by others but still feeling the pain of loneliness.

I remember feeling like this for a number of years, although I was married and had many friends, I found it difficult to go beyond surface level. After a while, I'm sure it became a normal feeling and I had no idea what to do about it anyway, but then I attended a School of Ministry in Toronto, Canada, and heard a teaching entitled 'Hearts of stone.' I was hooked … here was my condition and what to do about it! You can imagine my relief! However, I have also found that it wasn't just a teaching for me, it's something that affects us all and we continuously have to be aware of the possible stony areas of our hearts.

The concept of a stony heart is in the Bible. In the book of Ezekiel it says: "I will give them an undivided heart and put a new spirit in them, I will remove from them their heart of stone and give them a heart of flesh." (11:19 NIV)

God wants you to have a soft heart to receive from Him, to hear His voice and to enjoy your relationship with Him and with others. The world tells you a different story, "You have to protect yourself,' and "Look after number one first." I remember a pop song I liked when I was growing up called "Victim of Love". The lead singer would blast out the words to the chorus, "I'm building a wall, every day it's getting higher, I don't want to be another victim of love." We think this makes sense to our logical brains but it's choosing to take down those bricks around our hearts one by one, that will lead to freedom.

You may be reading this and thinking that it applies to you and wondering how you started to put that shield around your heart. It can begin at a young age, even in the most 'normal' of families when, as a child, you didn't get your own way, you were misunderstood or didn't get the attention you wanted. I don't think that we start out consciously putting up walls, but it becomes an auto response to keep us from getting hurt again.

I was born into a family with an older brother, and then me, until I was seven years old when my twin brother and sister were born and my world was turned upside down. Then there was the church, and ministry responsibilities for my parents and in my eyes, there was little time and attention left for me. It's not a blame game, it's the process of recognizing where the pain began and what caused you to start shutting off your heart.

As I'm sharing, I'd encourage you to think about what your home was like when you were growing up. Healing comes to our hearts when we recognize our true feelings, forgive those who hurt us and repent for our actions of shutting others out of our lives.

Sometimes we like to think it's someone else's problem. "What's wrong with them?", when usually we need to look into our own hearts. I innocently thought that once I'd married Mr. Right and got my own home, I would do things differently and they would be much better. Let me tell you, it doesn't work like that, you get married and you inherit someone else's baggage too. It's much better to allow the Lord to work in your heart, bring His healing, and relationships will become easier.

It's good to become familiar with your own feelings because each day as you walk through life your heart gets affected, someone might ignore you, not include you or cancel on you. It's best to acknowledge how you feel, forgive them and move on. You'll notice me talking about forgiveness a lot but that's because it's a very powerful tool and it really will help you to keep your heart soft and to move on from the wounds of the past.

Don't forget that the Bible says that laughter is good for the heart, it's like a good medicine that helps you to enjoy life and puts other issues into perspective. Make sure you take a good laughter tonic every day, it's good for your spiritual and your physical health.

ACTION STEP

Think about what your home was like growing up. There may have been times when you felt lonely, hurt or unsafe. Spend a few minutes forgiving anyone who made you feel like that. Ask God to help you to take away the shield from around your heart and to trust Him to protect you.

VERSE OF THE DAY

"A merry heart does good like medicine."

Proverbs 17:22

Chapter 17

What's Your Weakness?

If you've been involved in a job search recently and done some prep work, you'll know that this is one question that is likely to come up in the interview. You'll also know that you can google an acceptable answer for this question and then convince your interviewer that you're an accomplished perfectionist who is working towards having a spirit of excellence.

It is a tricky one though because who wants to talk about their faults and failures? I started my current administrative position this past year and now, as I realize that it's an all-encompassing role, I should have mentioned that manual projects are not my strong point, but with the help of YouTube and some advice from Jonathan, it's an area I'm growing in.

It's good to know yourself. The Bible tells us that God is familiar with all our ways and He knows us better than we know ourselves. This is a relief to me because sometimes I can ask Him why I'm feeling a certain way and He gives me some insight. That's the good news … the bad news is that the Enemy knows us too, he studies you for weak spots and he has a unique strategy against you.

How does this work? He knows our weak areas and he tries to tempt us with some bait, then it's up to us whether or not we take the bait and fall into temptation. Think about temptation for a minute, we're not all tempted by the same things. You could bring a box of donuts and they're not going to tempt me, but bring the cheesecake and some European chocolates … and anything salted caramel, now we're talking!!! I think you get my point!

Last year I attended a health seminar and heard one of the speakers saying that you should take your own bottle of water to a social function and then, to keep two hands on the wheel so that you're not tempted by the drinks and nibbles. In that way you won't blow all your health goals on one occasion.

This concept of keeping two hands on the wheel has stuck with me, to be prepared in advance for the temptations to come and having a strategy to win the battle. It's a concept that you can carry over to the spiritual realm, to be prepared for the attacks of the Enemy, because they will come. He is no gentleman; he doesn't fight fair and he'll certainly try to take you out when you're down.

One of my favorite stories on spiritual warfare is the battle between David and Goliath. I mean, who doesn't love this one? And that's because our good guy, the underdog, wins every time you read the story.

Let's start by setting the scene. You have two armies facing each other, the Israelites and their arch enemy the Philistines. But the battle is going nowhere because every day the giant champion of the Philistines comes out and puts forth a challenge to one of the Israelite army to come and fight him. The Israelites take one look at this brute and they're all quivering in their boots. It doesn't matter what reward they might win, no one wants to fight him. This same scenario continues for forty days until our little shepherd boy, the unlikely hero, shows up and takes on the challenge.

It's such a familiar story but I was reading it one day and the Lord opened my eyes to show me the Enemy's tactics. Just like Goliath, Satan will taunt us with the same line day after day. We just need to recognize the line that he's feeding us and start to reject his lies. What has he been telling you? Like I said, it will be different for us all but perhaps some of these lines sound familiar: "You're not good enough", "You're not gonna make it", "You're gonna end up alone", and so it goes on and on.

Whatever it is, we need to learn to respond like David did, shut him up and tell him some truth, "How dare you talk like that to the child of the King!"

It doesn't matter whether the Enemy comes at you with thoughts and lies or a more physical temptation, maybe trying to lure you into the well-known vices such as sex, drugs, alcohol. All these things will ultimately lead you away from God, that's why it's best to stay away from them, but whatever it is, the winning strategy is still the same.

If you think about David, he said that he took on Goliath because he had previously fought a lion and a bear while looking after sheep. Think back on some times when God has really helped you or come through for you and encourage your own faith with these testimonies. If you've not got any in your own victory arsenal, encourage yourself with someone else's stories until you have your own.

Another way I prepare for battle is to have what I call, a 'go to verse', it's one that the Lord has often led me to whenever I've been going through a difficult situation. This same verse brings me comfort and peace and the Lord takes me back there time and time again.

ACTION STEP

Be honest with yourself and think about your weaknesses and deepest fears. Allow the Lord to minister His healing in these areas and be patient, healing is a journey and it all takes time.

Write down your own 'go to verse'. You can use mine if you like, I will share it willingly but whichever verse you choose, write it out and memorize it so that you always have it ready.

_____

_____

My 'go to verse' is our **VERSE OF THE DAY**

"Trust in the Lord with all your heart and lean not on your own understanding. In all your ways submit to him and he will make your paths straight."

Proverbs 3:5-6 NIV

Chapter 18

We All Need A Rest Day

We live in a very busy world and you may feel that you're on the go all the time. Even when you get to sit down, you may feel that you're not really resting, you're thinking about everything you have to do and all the people you have to see.

Rest is so important for the human body. All good athletes know that they need to put in some rest days among their workouts because muscles need time to repair and grow and then the athlete can improve their overall performance.

In the book of Genesis at the very beginning of the Bible you can read the story of creation and how God spent six days creating the universe and all that's in it and He rested on the seventh day. He wanted to set a principle for us to follow, to spend one day each week in rest, rejuvenation and to set aside some time to dedicate to Him.

There's a powerful little story in the New Testament that shows that Jesus had the same attitude towards rest. If you turn to Luke 10:38-42, you can read about Jesus going to visit His friends, who are called Mary and Martha (and they also have a brother named Lazarus). If you can, try and imagine yourself in this scene. Martha welcomes Jesus into their home, and she starts to serve Him. This was probably what was expected of her at the time, you have to remember that women didn't have equal rights, their place was most likely to have been in the kitchen. According to the expectations of the day and to her sister, Martha, this is what Mary should have been doing also. But as Jesus started to talk, something captivated Mary and she sat at Jesus' feet and listened to what He was saying.

I'm sure that as Mary sat there she felt the pull of the expectation, maybe the huffing and puffing of her sister as she was serving alone, maybe even the silent thoughts of the disciples or the other men in the room, that she shouldn't be sat there with them, but there was something about Jesus' presence that kept her at His feet.

Jesus knew all about the expectations of Mary's day and He knows about all the responsibilities on your shoulders. When Martha became so exasperated with her sister, she finally exploded to Jesus, "This isn't right, tell my sister to come and help me in the kitchen." Jesus didn't respond like any other man would have, he simply told her that she was worked up over many things but that Mary had chosen the better way.

Sometimes it's hard to strike a balance between working, serving and resting and all the other things that we need to fit in, in between, but Jesus is concerned about our hearts and our relationships. It's only when we spend some time in stillness and invite His presence that we're truly able to hear from Him, just like Mary did.

This could have been an insignificant little story in the Bible, you can summarize it by saying that Jesus went to visit two sisters and they had an argument because one of them didn't help in the kitchen and Jesus took her side. However, the concept of taking time out from the busyness is so important to Jesus and He loves it when we prioritize our time with Him. That's the only way we'll grow in our relationship with Him.

I know that I used to find it hard to rest, it was easier to be busy than to be confronted with some of the pain that was hidden in my heart. If I was occupied all the time, then I didn't need to deal with it and I could pretend that it wasn't there. I remember in the earlier days of our marriage, Jonathan would say to me, "Can you just sit down!" I'm sure he's not the only husband who's ever said those words and I'm sure that the Father was saying the same thing to me. He was also crying out for intimacy.

My pace of life changed when I left England and went to attend a five-month School of Ministry. I was expecting a full paced ministry schedule rushing from service to service, feeling on FIRE but I found that it was a slow pace with times set aside to deal with the issues of my heart and allow the Father to pour in His healing.

One of the activities that we were taught to do was called 'soaking', which is basically just spending time in the Father's presence doing nothing except receiving from Him. You have to get into a comfortable position, put on some restful or instrumental music and invite Father God to come with His presence and speak His thoughts into your heart and mind. At the beginning this was so difficult for me, my thoughts would keep wandering on to something else, but I just had to keep bringing them back again and learning the discipline of rest. Just like anything else, with practice and also with the healing that I was receiving in my heart, it became easier for me to do. This was exactly what I needed, and I am so thankful for my time at the school.

Our Father knows how weary you are, what burdens you carry around, the times you try to put them down and pick them right back up again, He wants to give you complete rest for your body, soul and spirit.

I want to encourage you to be like Mary, to ignore the distractions and spend some time just sitting at the Father's feet. It's something that you'll do by faith, just like I did when I first learned about soaking. During this time you can tell Him how you feel, you can read the Bible, listen to some worship music, but make sure you give Him time to speak to you and to minister to your heart. You will come away feeling more refreshed and strengthened to face whatever life is bringing at that moment.

ACTION STEP

Whenever you're feeling tired of life, think about this verse and receive the rest that Jesus wants to give you.

_____

_____

VERSE OF THE DAY

Then Jesus said, "Come to me, all of you who are weary and carry heavy burdens, and I will give you rest. Take my yoke upon you. Let me teach you, because I am humble and gentle at heart, and you will find rest for your souls."

Matthew 11:28-29 NLT

Chapter 18

Help! I Don't Know How To Pray!

If you feel like this, then don't worry, you're in good company; the disciples had to ask Jesus how to pray. They had been with Jesus 24/7 for a couple of years, had been sent out into ministry and still weren't sure how to pray effectively. What they did know was that they saw Jesus praying to the Father and they wanted Jesus to share His secrets with them. This is when Jesus taught them to pray what we know as 'The Lord's prayer' or the 'Our Father', so once again it's just the concept of communicating with Father God.

So why then, has it become so complicated and why do we find it so difficult? Here's where we'll look at some of the issues that may be messing with your prayer life.

You may feel that you simply don't know what to say. You may listen to other people praying in church, or nowadays, on YouTube and they seem to pray so eloquently with the words just flowing off the tongue. I may be one of those people that you've heard and I have to admit that it's a lot easier these days, I just open my mouth and speak out whatever is on my heart or mind.

Years ago though it wasn't like that, I had no confidence to pray out loud and used to rehearse my prayer in my mind before I would ever say anything and then hope fervently that I wouldn't lose my train of thought in the middle of the prayer.

Obviously, that was my experience praying in a group setting but I think you can have the same issue when it's just you on your own. Let's get this straight though, God just wants to hear from you! There's no specific vocabulary that you need to use or a special voice, like you're talking to someone important on the telephone ... and you know if you're guilty of having a phone voice! Just speak to Him like you're talking to a friend or a brother and be confident that He hears you; what's important to you is important to Him.

Well maybe you know there's no specific way to talk to God, but you've not done it in a while and you're just not sure how to start again. Yes, I've been there too, it feels like you've got a whole mountain to climb before you can talk to Him again. But that's just not true. The Enemy wants to keep you out of relationship with the Heavenly Father, but He knows exactly where you are and is simply waiting for you to come back to Him.

If you're feeling like this, you may also be aware of some sin in your life. Just take care of it, repent and ask God to forgive you and stop doing it, it's as simple as that. Jesus already paid the price for your sin so that you can have that relationship with a Holy God.

There's also the possibility that you're disappointed in God. You prayed and believed for something and it didn't come to pass. You feel like your prayers are just hitting the ceiling, so why bother? This is where you have to trust God, forgive Him and release Him from your judgement of what He did or didn't do.

Isaiah 55:8-9 says: "For My thoughts are not your thoughts, Nor are your ways My ways," says the Lord. "For as the heavens are higher than the earth, So are My ways higher than your ways, And My thoughts than your thoughts."

This is where you trust that God sees the whole picture and He knows more than you do and as you pray about something, you leave the result in His hands.

So, wherever you're at spiritually, I want to encourage you to start praying regularly. Just think of it as communication with a God who loves you infinitely. Be sure not to complicate things, and try not to just read off a list of needs to Him, He wants to hear from your heart.

Jesus gave the disciples a model prayer that has lasted through the ages and it provides a good example to follow. When you pray include some worship of God for who He is and thank Him for what He's done before you ask for your requests. You can pray for your own needs, for friends, family and situations near and far.

You can pray anywhere, at any time, you don't have to schedule a time and place. The Bible says to pray without ceasing, which to me means that you should just stay in continual communication with God throughout the day, wherever you are and whatever you're doing. If you get distracted and your thoughts start wandering, don't give up, just bring your thoughts back and get back to your prayer, this still happens to me!

The most important thing is to make sure you pray. Be confident that God hears you and He answers you, it may just not be in the timing or the way that you expect. Prayers are powerful, so make praying a habit and expect to see situations change all around you!

ACTION STEP

Think about where you're at and commit to a new season of prayer today. Don't forget to write down what you're praying and the answers you receive!

VERSE OF THE DAY

"In this manner, therefore, pray: "Our Father in heaven, hallowed be your name. Your kingdom come, your will be done, on earth as it is in heaven. Give us this day our daily bread, and forgive us our debts, as we forgive our debtors. And do not lead us into temptation, but deliver us from the evil one."

Matthew 6:9-13

Chapter 20

What Is The Full Armor?

When Dr. Alicia was first starting her practice in Gulf Shores she would teach at different associations, churches and clubs about the armor or tools that God has given us to protect ourselves and to lead a healthy life. The tools she talked about were eating a nutritious diet, getting sufficient exercise, chiropractic care, essential oils and a non-toxic life style, and the importance of faith and a spiritual life.

While I agree with all of these and incorporate them all into my own way of life, my faith and spiritual life are by far the most important for me. The other tools will impact our quality of life in the here and now but it's salvation through Jesus and faith in Him that will affect our eternal destiny. Life on this earth is so short compared to eternity.

The Apostle Paul wrote about the armor of God in his letter to the Ephesians. It may seem a little bit strange for us to think about getting dressed for battle every day if we live near the beach, in the country or in the city but Paul wrote at a time when the Romans occupied most of the known world. Every day the 1st century Christians would see Roman soldiers dressed for battle, ready to protect their empire at any moment. They wore six specific pieces of armor that were proven for battle and these are what Paul picked out for us to wear as protection in the spiritual battle that we face continuously.

As we look at each piece of armor let me start off by saying that you have to wear them all for complete protection, it's not a case of deciding what you're going to wear each day, picking and choosing each item. The truth is that we are in a spiritual war, there are forces of good and evil, darkness and light, we have an enemy who is warring against us, who wants to steal, kill, and destroy our lives, but Jesus has won the ultimate victory and has provided the tools that we need to take up and use on a daily basis.

As we quickly go through each piece of armor, I want you to try to visualize it, put it on and think about how it can protect you in any struggle that you're going through.

The Belt of Truth

In Biblical times, men wore long robes with a belt around the middle. When they needed to run or work, they would hitch up their robe and stuff it into the belt to have more mobility, so it wouldn't get caught up and they could move quickly. I certainly understand what outfits are good for workouts and which are more suitable for formal occasions where you don't have to move around too much!

The belt would also cover the waist or the bowels of a person, which is where our emotions are stored in the body. It is important for us to stand on the truth, not get caught up in unimportant stuff and not be controlled by our emotions!

Biblical truth is so important, it's what sets us free. Think about your situation right now, are there any truths that will help you to fight? Write them down in the space below.

_____

The Breastplate of Righteousness

The breastplate was attached to the belt and reached up to the neck. It protected the heart, the one key organ responsible for sending blood through the circulatory system to keep us alive. Our spiritual lives can deaden if our hearts are not right with God.

I think that the Devil wants us to feel like we're good-for-nothing sinners and many times he succeeds. But it's not about you and what you've done, it's all about accepting what Jesus did on the cross for you. This is probably the most freeing thing in the world!

The Shoes of Peace

The Romans wore heavy leather sandals with iron hobnails hammered into the soles which allowed the soldiers to inflict damage on their enemy, even with their shoes.

Put your shoes on and keep them on so you're always ready for battle. Jesus gives us His peace which is deep, supernatural and you can't even understand it but it can keep you grounded no matter what life throws at you.

The Helmet of Salvation

Just like it did for a Roman soldier, a well-designed helmet will protect you from various angles of attack. The Enemy usually tries to attack our mind with his lies and he's very subtle because he puts thoughts in our heads that we think are our own. We need to pay attention to what's going on in our mind because what starts as thoughts, can easily become actions, or a lack of them.

Be active and make sure you're thinking about what you're thinking about. Are there any thoughts that you need to change to make them agree with the truth of the Bible? How would Jesus respond to your thoughts?

The Shield of Faith

This was in addition to the pieces of clothing. It was approximately 4 x 2 feet and it protected the soldier from his knees to his chin. Groups of soldiers would come together and hold their shields to protect the group. The shield allowed a soldier to advance even when the enemy was attacking him.

The Romans used to rub their shields with oil so that the arrows would slip off. Oil in the Bible is symbolic of the Holy Spirit, if you stay filled with the Holy Spirit, the fiery arrows of the evil one will not be able to harm you.

The Enemy may be throwing some darts at you right now but keep your faith in God, that He is who He says He is and He will do what He says He will do. Use that as your shield and eventually all the arrows will slip off.

The Sword of the Spirit

The Roman soldier's sword was a powerful deadly weapon that was intended to kill. It was a double-edged sword that cut in two directions. You may have heard that the Word of God (the Bible) is also described as a double-edged sword. If you use it, meditate on it and speak it forth, it can be a powerful weapon for any battle that you are facing and it can do some serious damage in the enemy's camp.

Finally ... Pray

Pray in the Spirit on all occasions with all kinds of prayers and requests. Paul frequently talks about the importance of regular prayer for yourself, others, people you know and people you don't. Prayer can affect situations and destinies, don't ever underestimate the importance of prayer. Short quick prayers, long laborious prayers, loud and fiery or soft and quiet prayers, God hears them all, they are all powerful.

As we've gone through the pieces of armor, think about how important each piece is. Once you've done everything you can, remember to stand firm, you're not fighting on your own. We go through seasons that are more intense than others, stand firm, put on the armor of God and you will get through this season.

ACTION STEP

Be sure to read and meditate on Paul's instructions on the Full Armor in Ephesians 6.

_____

_____

VERSE OF THE DAY

"Put on the Full Armor of God so that you can stand against the devil's schemes."

Ephesians 6:11 NIV

Chapter 21

What Kind Of Trail Are You Leaving?

As we're coming to the end of this devotional, I wanted to finish with a thought about the kind of trail that we leave behind us.

If you go down to the beach at Gulf Shores, you'll hear or see the slogan, "Leave only footprints," because as locals we don't enjoy it when visitors leave undesirable items on our beaches but we like to see a trail of footprints. Of course, there are other trails we can leave. Jonathan loves to wear cologne and he's famous for it too, sometimes even if I can't see him, I know that he's been around because I can smell his favorite cologne in the air!

Have you ever thought about a spiritual trail? This is an example that you can leave for others to follow. It's a concept that God put on my heart when we went on a two-month physical journey in South America in 2016. As we traveled from Chile to Peru to Ecuador and back to Chile again, we stayed in different people's homes and ministered in so many different churches. We saw lives being touched, some physical healings and maybe a few salvations, but you always wonder what impact you're having in ministry or just in life in general. That's when the Lord gave me the impression that we were depositing spiritual treasure into peoples' lives and as we traveled from place to place we were leaving a spiritual trail behind us for others to follow.

It's a concept that I got from Paul the Apostle as I was reading his letters to Timothy. I'm sure that when Paul was writing all his letters in the 1st century, he had no idea of the extent of the impact they would have and yet they still speak life to us, here in the 21st century.

These are Paul's words to Timothy in 2 Timothy 3 :10: "But you have carefully followed my doctrine, manner of life, purpose, faith, long-suffering, love, perseverance ..." He also goes on to talk about persecutions, and I don't like to think about this too much, but we know that Paul suffered a lot of persecutions for the sake of the Gospel but he also says here, that the Lord delivered him out of them all.

However, this was the trail Paul had left for his spiritual son to follow, which would set Timothy apart from the crowd and cause him to be successful in his own journey. I want to take a look at some of the gemstones that Paul left on his path for us to uncover.

Doctrine - what do you believe and how does it affect your life?

I don't really use this word a lot but it's good to know what you believe and live according to it. I think that my life has mostly been impacted by our church's FIRE values which is an acrostic for: Father's love, Intimacy and Hearing God's voice, Restoration of the Heart and Soul, Experiencing the Holy Spirit. These four values and the concepts they contain, have really changed my life.

Manner of Life

We're not to be conformed to this world and sometimes that means sacrificing our own rights and desires to become a sweet-smelling fragrance to the Lord and the world around us. It may mean being sweet to the Walmart cashier or the server in a restaurant when the wait time has been exceptionally long or it may mean not getting involved in the office gossip. It will be different whatever stage of life you're in but remember that just as Timothy watched Paul, other people watch how we live. Make sure you leave them an example to follow.

Purpose

We all need a purpose, it's what helps us to get out of bed in the morning and keeps us moving forward. Some people have a strong sense of purpose, while others like me feel like we're just called to let our light shine wherever we are.

Faith

This will enable you to do what God has called you to do, knowing that He will go before you and back you up. Faith is definitely an anchor in every situation.

Long suffering

The definition of this word quite literally is suffering long … don't you just love that one? It's one of God's qualities and how He feels towards us. He loves us, He's gracious and compassionate and slow to anger. This is how He wants us to act in our relationships with one another.

Love

Ooh, this one is harder that it sounds. Some people are easier to love than others but that just means that we have to be even more intentional about loving these folks!

Perseverance

I feel like this has been my word for a very long season, I always seem to be pushing through something, so maybe this is just life! Look at this Biblical definition of perseverance: "The capacity to continue to bear up under difficult circumstances, not with passive complacency but with hopeful fortitude that actively resists weariness and defeat."

Now when I read that it makes me feel proud of my accomplishments and it also tells me how much God values perseverance especially when it may be easier to give up.

If you're reading this, I want to congratulate you for persevering through to the end of this journey and to encourage you to keep going. No matter what life throws at you, continue to walk forward, to persevere, to know that God is with you and that you can do all things through Him who strengthens you.

ACTION STEP

Think about the trail that you're leaving behind you and write below the gemstones that you want others to find in your path.

_____

_____

VERSE OF THE DAY

"But you have carefully followed my doctrine, manner of life, purpose, faith, long-suffering, love, perseverance …". 2 Timothy 3:10.

Forgiving Prayer

I have prayed this prayer many, many times and have found that it is an invaluable tool to keep my heart soft toward others. It's so simple yet powerful and I encourage you to pray it regularly too.

Lord, I forgive _____

I give you permission to take the judgment and bitterness out of my heart. I do not want this in my life. I surrender it to You and ask You to remove it - to heal me where I have been wounded, to forgive me where I have sinned. I choose not to blame or hold the actions of _____ against them. I hereby surrender my right to be paid back for my loss by the one who has sinned against me, and in so doing, I declare my trust in God alone as the righteous Judge.

Father God, bless them in every way.

In Jesus' name, amen.

Taken from 'As We Forgive Those - How to Forgive Others, Ourselves and God' by Charles F. Finck and used with permission.

Final Thoughts

Well, we've come to the end of this part of our short journey together. Hopefully I've been able to answer at least one question you've been struggling with and also given you the confidence to keep trusting God and to keep moving forward. I understand that I've covered a wide range of topics here and only touched the surface on them. If I've uncovered more questions in your heart or you're wondering how your experience fits into the thoughts I've shared, please contact me at: **www.adevotionaljourney.com** I'd love to hear from you!

If you've noticed some recurring thoughts in this book, it's not that I like to be repetitive, it's likely because they have become the themes of my life. Forgiveness, healing of the heart, faith, trust, believe, pray, keep fighting, keep moving forward ... I'd encourage you to live by these words too!

Until next time ...

Esther Milne

*"Know where you are headed
and you will stay on solid ground."*

Taken from Proverbs 4:26

Made in the USA
Monee, IL
13 March 2022

92845891R00066